Oscar Remembered

Oscar Remembered

by

Maxim Mazumdar

Personal Library, Toronto

Personal Library
Suite 1607, 145 Marlee Avenue
Toronto, Canada M6B 3H3

Editor: Dorothy Martins
Designer: Don Fernley
Drawings: David Cyr

Although every effort was made to identify sources of quotations which appear in this work, the publishers would welcome any information about errors or omissions, which will be rectified in future editions.

Canadian Cataloguing in Publication Data
Mazumdar, Maxim, 1953-
    Oscar remembered
A play.
ISBN 0-920510-00-0 pa.
1. Wilde, Oscar, 1854-1900, in fiction, drama, poetry, etc. 2. Douglas, Alfred Bruce, Lord, 1870-1945, in fiction, drama, poetry, etc. I. Title.
PS8576.A98083   C812'.5'4   C77-001621-9
PR9199.3.M39083

Printed and bound in Canada

For W. S. McLean
This book, with love

Preface

Not since the great days of the Dominion Drama Festival has the accomplishment of a young actor won such attention. Maxim Mazumdar's adaptation and re-creation of a notorious Victorian literary scandal as a monodrama for himself so impressed leading Stratford actor, William Hutt, that he brought it to the attention of the Stratford Festival's new artistic director, Robin Phillips, as a presentation for Stratford's Third Stage. Winning Phillips' approval, Hutt then undertook to re-stage Mazumdar's work, *Oscar Remembered,* with the young playwright performing the role he created.

I saw it at Stratford as drama critic for *The Globe and Mail,* Toronto, and also approved Hutt's discovery. "Many new colours are added to Stratford's Festival and among the most vivid is *Oscar Remembered,* a transplant from a Montreal drama festival," I wrote for the next morning. "In its reminder of the fatal triangle of Wilde, the Marquis of Queensberry and his son, Lord Alfred Douglas, the 22-year-old Mazumdar, in fairytale terms, puts down Queensberry as the wicked ogre, Lord Alfred as the princess in the tower, and Wilde himself as the honest woodsman, labouring in the forest of art until led by the beloved into the trap set by the ogre."

The subject of Oscar Wilde's downfall has been heavily over-written since succeeding publics have come closer to an understanding of what was involved, of what Wilde's sin against the Victorian moral code actually involved. A noted Irish actor, Michéal MacLiammòir, had already given his one-man dramatization of Wilde at the Shaw Festival. One hardly felt the need of further illumination of the Irish poet-playwright's differences from the average husband and father of the period.

Mazumdar recaptured our interest in the subject by putting the spotlight on that hitherto rather pallid figure, Lord Alfred, whose alliance with Wilde had provoked the furious Queensberry. As Douglas was obviously the role Mazumdar felt best suited to, he made Wilde a shadowy figure in a wing-back chair, back to us, the mauve light coming and going, the green carnation on the chair arm rather than in the lapel. We gained another view of Wilde from the reflection in the countenance and voice of the young, gilded aristocrat facing us.

But Douglas was not shown in a favourable light here just because the playwright was also the performer. Indeed, his outburst, when Wilde dedicated the *Salomé* Douglas had translated to another, was enough to assure all your sympathy for the silent Wilde. His description of the ogre, his father, and his defiance of his mother, led you to seriously question Wilde's judgment in depending on Lord Alfred. Later, after Wilde has suffered incarceration and public ignomy, he explains why to those friends who are shocked when he rejoins the younger man. The reason is, simply, love, he says, and we must believe him.

In performance, the young monodramatist achieved genuine dramatic action, without which any kind of play is a failure. He dazzled us first with a view of Lord Alfred as a lush youth capable of both persuasion and demand, instead of a pale victim of a wicked poet. Then, as the evening progressed, he built up the other, the invisible, character until the pale shadow was revealed as an enobled victim of an enraged society.

Mazumdar achieves this fairly, quoting Wilde's own description of his half-hour of public shame on the platform of Clapham Junction. Then he follows this up with a reading of *De Profundis*, which the original Lord Alfred had condemned as the work of an evil and lying spirit. These two accounts, coupled with the simplicity of Wilde's statement of their romantic attachment, lifts Wilde nearer to sainthood than he has managed before in the most sympathetic of accounts. We do not hear Wilde's arrogance or his precious witticisms, you see.

This study of Wilde's martyrdom is a truly remarkable accomplishment for a 22-year-old Montrealer who found an audience beyond his local audience in the country's most eminent theatre, and beyond it into print. *Oscar Remembered* is an addition to the literature of the story of Oscar Wilde that is most certainly worth preserving.

Herbert Whittaker

Introduction

How exactly all the memories that create *Oscar Remembered* flooded together, I can never tell. Writing, even of any kind, is so inextricably linked with the sounds, smells, and influences of the passing moment that an exact genesis is impossible to render. Indeed why should one want to?

All I want is to somehow list the influences involved in the creation of this work in as few sentences as possible.

I was always a little bewitched by Wilde's influence – by his expansive style, his exotic images, his headlong fling with Life and Art. I think everybody loves that side of Wilde. *The Importance of Being Earnest,* his best and most popular work, is, after all, the importance of being accessible. And Laughter is a great Leveller. Everyone loves the play, the wit, the aphorisms, the perfect phrasing. Everyone is influenced by it in some way. *Perfect art.*

The human side of Wilde is less known and less accessible. Most people avoid the twisting ways of the human heart. And why not? Life's surface is troublesome enough to cope with. And yet, this was the side that meant the most to me. The vein of dark iron that prominently divided the valleys of gold and incense. There was subtle power in this vein.

The idea of doing a one-man entertainment on Wilde was most inviting because of the risk involved. What depth lay beneath the jewelled words, the conflicting biographies, the chameleon-like letters – this haunted me. And somewhere in the back of my mind, the elusive shadow of Bosie, Lord Alfred Douglas, darted elegantly in rondo figures.

Lord Alfred, Wilde's source of beauty and destruction, the golden god with the cloven hoof, or more prosaically, a talented, good-looking young aristocrat with a fascination for the gutter – somehow he fitted into the tapestry. It seemed right to remove him from the shelf of obscurity, from Wilde's shadow, and have him tell of their life together from his own point of view.

Oscar Remembered, in its first act, spans the relationship between this young lord and the older playwright from their initial meeting to just after Wilde's trials and conviction. The second act begins a few years after Wilde's death. Douglas is no longer young or beautiful; he is merely embittered and guilt-ridden. Slowly, through the reliving of Wilde's prison letter, his release from prison, their subsequent meetings, and that wonderful last poem *The Ballad of Reading Gaol,* Bosie accepts Wilde's death, exorcises his demons, and decides to start a new life for himself.

It has been suggested that *Oscar Remembered* makes of Bosie Douglas a more interesting character than his own life warrants. I disagree. Lord Alfred Douglas was a most mercurial character both in the objective orbit of art and the more subjective space of life, changeable as quicksilver, charming, gracious, and yet with a streak of madness ever-threatening to disturb the opalescent mirror of his surface. And in this there was a story to be told – something that I could impart some sensibility towards.

The idea was locked in crystal. With scarcely a sigh I discarded all thoughts of compiling the well-known Wilde, the brilliant but oft-quoted epigrams and catch phrases. Suddenly, there was no need to point out the success of his works – people could go to them easily enough. What they couldn't find easily was the heart of the man. And this was what I really wanted to chart – a human journey.

And how human it is. To this day, after several score performances, the thrill surging through Wilde's courtroom speech about the love that dare not speak its name still reverberates in my ear – Bosie's haunting and simple sonnet *The Dead Poet* is a most moving whisper. The echoes that surround *The Ballad of Reading Gaol,* the greatest of English ballads (in spite of S. T. Coleridge), are still compelling in their rhythms and passions. More so, in fact; familiarity and age do not wither Wilde's life and work or his love for Bosie. *Oscar Remembered* proves this to me.

Also the play has changed my life through a wonderful experience. Strangers can merge into friends. After a performance a curious phenomenon occurs – the audience is no longer anonymous, and artistic catharsis is no longer a lonely process. Somehow we have touched and are lifted away from ourselves to a realm where Wilde's and Douglas' whispers are no longer remote or shameful.

I owe a great deal to the hundreds of books written on Wilde and Douglas. Several charming expressions and phrases in the script owe much to the foundation suggested by others' work. I don't remember consciously who said what but I do feel a conscious debt to the million dancing words that deal with the subject exhaustively.

I remember reading the first draft of *Oscar Remembered,* as a rather precocious undergradute, to my life's teacher and dearest friend, Joanne Zuckerman. It was through her that I first felt the pulse of the work – its ebbs, its flows.

My friends William Thiess and Greg Peterson influenced the work through their endurance of my endless readings and countless questions. Their encouragement never waned even in the dark night of the soul when I felt like an artist with no art to speak of.

And William Hutt, Canada's foremost actor, gave such direction, love, and shape to my work as actor and writer that when I walked out onto the Stratford Stage in the flesh and soul of Bosie Douglas, August 16, 1975 (that most memorable of nights), I felt not in the least bit alone. There was respect, love, and purpose behind the pale loitering of Bosie's mauve shadow.

And I am surrounded by the best of companions and the best of works, and that in itself is a rare gift in our most ephemeral of arts.

Maxim Mazumdar
May 27, 1976
Montreal, Quebec

A Note on the Staging

The staging of *Oscar Remembered* is natural and simple, but in its very simplicity lies a challenge. It is no mean feat to keep an audience's attention for two hours, as there are only a certain number of visual patterns you can employ in a monologue. "Play with time and contrast the mood" – this dictum was constantly in William Hutt's mind. He was not afraid of stillness and not afraid of silence, two of the most important elements in his staging. He stripped away inessentials. Wilde's words and Bosie's memories were the focus. Hutt's design of movement, light, and mood served the focus.

He decided to drop the music that I had wanted to use as bridges between the scenes and to underline the script's mood. I was perturbed by this, but as usual he was right. The music of the words was enough. And we didn't need any "fill" – speed and attack are most essential in the performance of *Oscar*. These elements contrast with the languor of the times and word structure and provide a most exciting framework for the exotic and emotional material.

The furniture (I am thinking specifically of the Stratford production) consists of an enormous claret-coloured wing chair with Wilde's symbol, the green carnation, placed on it; beside it, a small side table adorned with an Art Deco bust of Apollo in pale grey marble. Across the expanse of stage floor stretches a rich looking Persian rug in hues of wine, blue, and gold. Past the rug is a writing desk and chair upholstered in royal blue velvet. The desk holds assorted properties: Bosie's letters, copies of *Salomé* and *Dorian Gray,* a decanter and glass on a silver tray and writing materials. A tall candle in an antique holder is the only other decoration on the desk. In the background stands a period telephone with its own table and chair. Further off to the side is a dark carved wooden screen with a lush fern in front of it. The fern is replaced before Act Two by a vase of dying roses.

The whole effect was that of a richly furnished drawing-room in which large spirits were free to roam. "Expressive realism" is my inadequate summing up of it.

The lighting in the play assumes the importance of a third character. It reflects fluid passages of time and intensity of moods.

"The Oscar Special," in a mysterious shade of lilac, appears on the wing chair that Oscar seems to occupy at various points in the evening, whenever his presence enters the drama. By careful operation, the light, creating shadows on the wing chair, fleshed out in my mind's eye a wonderful outline of Wilde – and this magic occurs every performance. There he sits, in lilac shadows, applauding a well-turned phrase or smiling and wagging a beringed finger when I hurt the rhythm of one of his observations.

I mention these details merely to illuminate visualization of the work. I hope these points succeed in working upon your imaginary forces.

M.M.

Oscar
Remembered

Act One

Scene One. The year is 1892. A pinspot cuts through the darkness to reveal the exquisite features of Lord Alfred Douglas. He smiles and slowly begins to speak in a dream-like tone that becomes more conversational as the scene progresses.

When I was little, my mother's name for me was Boysie, which I lisped into Bosie, and have never been able to get rid of it. I don't know now that I should want to really, but I must I suppose - certainly I must before I am old. But if you are right, and I am Dorian come to life, I needn't worry - to be like marvellous Dorian Gray, beauty lost in endless summer. And I am doubly lucky, for I'm sure I don't have his wicked heart.

The lights brighten gradually and reveal Bosie with a small silver tray bearing two cucumber sandwiches.

These cucumber sandwiches are delightful and very, very thin. If it isn't very, very thin, a cucumber sandwich is the grossest insult known to a truly sensitive palate. And you must positively not forget Oscar, some idle weekend, to write for me a play about cucumber sandwiches.

Bosie now turns to speak to Oscar, who seems to occupy the wing chair whenever it is lit with the "Oscar Special" as it is now.

You know what I really came to see you for. I don't know how to thank you. I asked you to help me because I felt instinctively that you were kind. You see, *Dorian Gray* indicated to me that in spirit, in temperament, in tastes, we were not unlike each other. And I needed a friend desperately. I was in trouble, and I knew how beastly, horrid and false, people are, how coarse and cruel. Oh I learned this repeatedly when I was still quite small, small and innocent. And if ever I was in danger of forgetting it, I was taught the same lesson by the same teacher. The Marquis of Queensberry. Yes, my father.

A child and a wife could not have a greater instructor in every form of brutality. His animal mind occupies itself constantly with an anxious search for new ways to make us miserable. He would have been in ecstasies to hear from that monster - the swine trying to rent me. My father would have sent off letters about it to my mother, my sister, and brothers - disgusting, poisonous letters. And he would have grinned all over his ape's face as he cut me off.

> *Suddenly Bosie's vengeful expression changes. He smiles.*

But you saved me. You are a saint, Oscar. And you look ever so faintly puzzled. Do tell what he was like? The swine renting me. You must have had to deal with him to get rid of him. Of course you aren't familiar with the expression "rent" are you? You don't make a habit of dealing with blackmailers. Have this last sandwich. Are you sure?

> *Bosie pops the sandwich into his own mouth. He continues very casually.*

Let us imagine that we are naked, and I am in your arms, and you are kissing me. Somebody knocks on the door, gives it a tremendous push, it flies open. A horrible man is there, with a little assistant as witness, and he threatens to go to the police, or to my father, or your wife, unless we give him what he wants. *This* is called renting us. Oh I should love to see his face as he opens my letter. I gave the monster back his own poison. There is enough filth in it to make even his thick hide sting. I sent it to him the minute I received your blessed note telling me you had taken care of it all.

Bosie puts down the tray on the side table beside Oscar's chair.

Must we go on from here to see Robbie Ross? Oh I am sure he is very nice, but he must learn to *share* you with others. Send him a note. Then we can stay here comfortably for the evening. Shall we? I should like to.

Bosie smiles at Oscar as the lights dim slightly to indicate the passage of time.

Scene Two. The year is 1893. Bosie crosses the stage, picks up a cigarette box and fishes out a gold-tipped cigarette as the lights brighten. Bosie excitedly addresses the audience.

I have just spent the weekend with them – and I met his wife, Constance, for the first time. She is pretty and good, but it would have been torment to have been surrounded by her domestic virtue for the entire weekend. Fortunately, there was Oscar.

After dinner on Saturday, Oscar said: "Bosie, you represent the youth and beauty in all my work. There is much in my art that is based upon your life. However, I have taken a great liberty and have made you a character

23

in my new play. The play is called *A Woman of No Importance,* and is all about a good woman and a bad man who is called Lord Illingworth. Naturally Illingworth is the hero of the play. I'm afraid there isn't very much of you, because if there were, you would steal the whole thing and demolish the plot. In order to confuse the critics hopelessly, I have called you – Lord Alfred – the best disguise is none at all."

I was delighted, naturally, but I wanted to know if I was to be allowed to smoke gold-tipped cigarettes onstage. Oscar nodded.

> *With great relish, Bosie dramatises this scene using different voices to create separate characterizations.*

A character in the play, Lady Stutfield, says, "How very charming those gold-tipped cigarettes of yours are Lord Alfred." And I reply: "They are awfully expensive. I can only afford them when I'm in debt." Then Lady Stutfield says: "It must be distressing to be in debt." But I correct her: "One must have some occupation nowadays. If I hadn't my debts, I shouldn't have anything to think about." "But," she asks, "don't the people to whom you owe money give you a great, great deal of annoyance?" "Oh good heavens, no," I reply, "they write, *I* don't."

> *Bosie laughs and lights a cigarette. He moves centre stage to perform the next section.*

Oscar is so wickedly perceptive. At that point the conversation began to mellow and I remember Oscar, although using the words of Lord Illingworth from his play, was somehow telling me something about himself. "Don't be afraid, dear boy. Remember that you have got on your side, the most wonderful thing in the world – youth! There is nothing like youth. The middle-aged are mortgaged to life. The old are in Life's lumber room. But

youth is the Lord of life. Youth has a kingdom waiting for it. To get back my youth, there is nothing in the world I wouldn't do - except get up early, take exercise, or be a useful member of the community."

I laughed because it sounded so like Oscar himself. Oscar laughed when I told him that. "My dear boy," he said, "how absurd. *I* take exercise, *I* get up early. And listen to Lord Illingworth on marriage, can you conceive *me* talking like this?

" 'Twenty years of romance make a woman look like a ruin; but twenty years of marriage make her something like a public building. Men marry because they are tired; women because they are curious. Both are disappointed. When one is in love one begins by deceiving oneself. And one ends by deceiving others. That is what the world calls a romance. But a really *grande passion* is comparatively rare nowadays. It is the privilege of people who have nothing to do. That is the one use of the idle classes in a country, and the only possible explanation of us Harfords. That is my family name. You should study the Peerage, dear boy. It is the one book a young man about town should know thoroughly, and it is the best thing in fiction the English have ever done'."

Then Oscar stopped and looked at me with a strange smile. Quietly, as himself, not Lord Illingworth, he said: "Among most people there is simply not the capacity for romance, they are too trivial, too shallow. How sad for them. For in life, nothing is really serious . . . except passion."

Bosie extinguishes his cigarette slowly as the lights fade, dissolving the scene.

Scene Three. Bosie moves to a period telephone, picks it up and begins to speak to his mother who is apparently on the other end of the line. The lights brighten.

Have I ever tried to make you think that *any* of my friends were *good*? I've consistently protested against dividing people into good and bad.

Well I admire good men just as you do.

Of course I see that a good man can be a splendid creature, but it was not you who taught me to see that, mother, it was simply Oscar.

How can he ruin my soul? I don't believe I had a soul before I met him.

What do you mean . . . what do you mean by "eccentric and peculiar views of morality"? They are not a special characteristic of my own, I know them

to have been shared by nearly all the great minds in ancient and modern times.

I did not imbibe those ideas from Oscar and he did not put them into my head.

Bosie shakes his head vehemently.

He does *not* encourage them! I had formed them in my own mind, and become quite certain of their truth before I ever met him or heard of him.

On the contrary, it was the finding of someone with a really great mind and genius who agreed with *me* that made me like him, and since then I have had more influence on him than he on me.

I didn't expect you to believe it.

There is a long silence while Bosie listens to his mother's diatribe on the other end of the line. Suddenly he laughs.

Now do get out of your head, this absurd idea about the ruin of my soul. Mother, Oscar and I are merely ordinary people who are fond of each other, and very anxious to live together, peacefully and happily, without scenes and tragedies and reproaches.

Oh do be a little more commonplace, and a little less emotional.

I'm aware of that. I know that I have in my blood the love of a scene and a tragedy. There is a tendency in all of us to lift everything onto the stilts of tragedy, but somebody, in our family of all families, ought to make a determined stand against it. We are all so theatrical. Let us cease and become a little bourgeois.

Well, what do you propose to give me in exchange for this man. Where am I to go for my quickening? Who is going to transpose me out of this tedious world into a land of paradox and beauty?

Bosie is beginning to get visibly upset.

I think that when Oscar's life comes to be written, our friendship will be written about as one of the most beautiful things in the world, as beautiful as the love of Shakespeare and the unknown Mr. W.H., or Plato and Socrates.

Neither you nor anyone has the right to say that he is a bad man. A really bad man I could never love. And what is more, he could never love me, as faithfully and as purely, as does Oscar. Believe me, there is nothing so ludicrous as the one-sided point of view of a mother. It is always *her* son who is being led astray, it is always the others who are brutes and blackguards. Please try and like my friend who is so dear to me.

Mother! . . .

He is too upset to continue speaking.

Well I cannot say any more now. Goodbye.

Angrily, he hangs up. The lights dim.

Scene Four. Bosie moves to the port decanter on his desk and pours himself a glass of wine. The lights come up. Bosie's mood has vanished with the previous scene. He is now the charming, gracious host who has just given an intimate dinner party for two of his chums at Oxford, Campbell and

Taylor. The "Oscar Special" is up, for Oscar too, has been present. In the scene Bosie addresses several remarks to two areas of the room where his friends are standing. He begins the scene reciting the last quatrain from his own poem, Two Loves, *a work that shocked the conventional Victorian minds of the day.*

I am true Love, I fill
The hearts of boy and girl with mutual flame.
Then sighing said the other, 'Have thy will,
I am the love that dare not speak its name'.

Bosie laughs delightedly and toasts the company in the room.

Thank you my dear friends, and you, Oscar. The dinner was charming, and the company quite perfect. Welcome to this Grecian celebration of Poesy and Pleasure. Will you have some coffee now? I can ask Alfred to bring it in here. What, nobody? Well then you must have a cigarette, while I come to the last part of my readings.

He moves around the room offering each one a cigarette, still speaking.

You know, a cigarette is like a work of Oscar's. It is the perfect type of a perfect pleasure. It is exquisite and it leaves one unsatisfied. What more could one want?

He picks up a book which contains The Harlot's House *and* The Picture of Dorian Gray.

I love acting. It is so much more real than life. I have known everything, but I am always ready for a new emotion. And Oscar's works of sin contain the rarest feelings.

And he begins to recite, becoming more and more involved in the languid decadence of the poem.

THE HARLOT'S HOUSE

We caught the tread of dancing feet
We loitered down the moonlit street
And stopped beneath the harlot's house.

Inside above the din and fray
We heard the loud musicians play
The 'Treues Liebes Herz' of Strauss.

Like strange mechanical grotesques,
Making fantastic arabesques,
The shadows raced across the blind.

We watched the ghostly dancers spin
To sound of horn and violin
Like black leaves wheeling in the wind.

Sometimes a clockwork puppet pressed
A phantom lover to its breast
Sometimes they seemed to try to sing.

Sometimes a horrible marionette
Came out, and smoked its cigarette
Upon the steps like a live thing.

Then turning to my love, I said,
"The dead are dancing with the dead,
The dust is whirling with the dust."

But he, he heard the violin
And left my side and entered in:
"Love passed into the house of Lust."

Then suddenly the tune went false,
The dancers wearied of the waltz,
The shadows ceased to wheel and whirl.

And down the long and silent street,
The dawn with silver sandalled feet,
Crept like a frightened girl.

*Bosie moves across the room and sits in a chair
beside the telephone while reciting the following
passages. Lights change subtly to enhance the
mood of each piece. The stagelights have dimmed
considerably, the brightest spots being reserved for
Bosie and the light on Oscar's chair.*

When I re-read the book of my radiant sin, *Dorian Gray,* a curious image
rose before my eyes, it suddenly struck me that Basil Hallward, the painter,
had walked off the pages and become Oscar describing *our* first meeting:

"I turned halfway round and saw Dorian Gray for the first time. When our eyes
met I felt that I was growing pale. A curious instinct of terror came over me. I
knew that I had come face to face with someone whose mere personality was so
fascinating that, if I allowed it to do so, it would absorb my whole nature.

Something seemed to tell me that I was on the verge of a terrible crisis in my life. I knew that fate had in store for me exquisite joys and exquisite sorrows. I knew that if I spoke to Dorian I would become absolutely devoted to him. He is all my art to me now. It is not merely that I paint from him, draw from him, model from him. Of course I have done all that. He is Paris and Adonis. He has leaned over the still pool of some Greek woodland, and seen in the water's silent silver the wonder of his own beauty. But he is much more to me than that. Unconsciously, he defines for me the lines of a fresh school, a school that is to have in itself all the passion of the romantic spirit, all the perfection of the spirit that is Greek."

And later, when he speaks directly to Dorian:

"It is quite true that I have worshipped you with far more romance of feeling than a man usually gives to a friend. Somehow I have never loved a woman. From the moment I met you, your personality had the most extraordinary influence over me. I quite admit that I adored you madly, extravagantly, absurdly. I was jealous of everyone to whom you spoke. I wanted to have you all to myself. I was only happy when I was with you. One day, I determined to paint a wonderful portrait of you. It was to have been my masterpiece."

> *There is a breathless hush in the room for a few seconds. Then Bosie springs up and crosses quickly to his desk.*

I have a wonderful surpise. Oscar knows about it, of course.

> *To Oscar.*

But you haven't told anyone have you?

> *He takes out a wrapped package from a desk drawer.*

Now you know that Oscar wrote *Salomé* in French. Well I have just finished the translation.

He laughs happily like a little child.

You didn't know *that* Oscar, did you? It is my gift to you. And this is Oscar's gift for me.

He holds aloft the package.

The first copy of *Salomé* has been rushed over from Paris

He opens the package and shows everyone the beautiful first edition of Salomé.

in its royal Tyrian robes and delectable rather tired silver, with Aubrey Beardsley's divine drawings. *Salomé,* par Oscar Wilde. Dedicated to –

He opens the book to the first page and is stunned by what he sees. Oscar Wilde dedicated the play to the young man who helped him compose it in French.

A mon ami, Pierre Louys.

There is an ominous silence in the room. Bosie turns away, his face working convulsively. He begins quietly, but by the end of the speech has worked himself into a terrible rage.

Your play is hideous. I said, quite hideous, Oscar. Your ears must be full of wax, or whatever the revolting stuff is that gets into them. You should have them cleaned out. You heard me, Campbell, didn't you? And you, Taylor? Never mind, I shall say it again. I said the play is quite hideous. It is quite HIDEOUS! Your maggot words, I spit from my lips. Hypocrite, loathsome, crawling, filthy creature. I can't bear hypocrisy, if there is one thing I cannot bear, it is hypocrisy. And you are the fat lord of all the hypocrites! Here, here are your poems and pretty plays –

He flings the copies of Dorian Gray, Harlot's House, *and* Salomé *into the wastepaper basket.*

- go, go to your Pierre Louys, nuzzle your face between his frog legs. Pederast, sodomite, you filthy bugger!

Screaming at the others

Sit down the lot of you till I have finished what I have to say.

He begins to laugh hysterically.

Look everyone, look, where his *fat greasy* fingers touched me.

He screams the words, almost foaming with rage. Wildly he points at his sexual parts . . .

Here . . . and here . . . and here!

He turns accusingly upon Oscar again

Betrayer . . . Oscariot . . . OSCARIOT!!!

All the lights snap out. There is only the faintest glimmer of light surrounding Bosie's desk. He moves quickly to light a candle on the desk. The spotlight illuminating the desk brightens. It is a few hours later. Bosie sits down shuddering. With shaking hands he pours himself a drink and gulps it down. The fiery liquid seems to quiet his trembling. He begins to write a letter.

My darling Oscar,

I beg you to forgive me. I was insane with jealousy. *Salomé* was mine. I am the Biblical princess of your art transfixed in our lives together. You told me of my symbolic progression through beauty in your art, in your life: *Dorian, Mr. W.H., Salomé*. It is not a hideous play. It is quite perfect and beautiful as you said. If it were not so beautiful it would not have hurt me so much. It *is* beautiful and it is *you*. I beg you to forgive me and come and join me here. I cannot come to join you with the others because it would be too painful. It would remind me of last night.

With *all* my love,
Bosie

Silence. Bosie stares ahead of him into the darkness. Then he speaks from the desk softly.

Oscar . . .

And the "Oscar Special" comes up slowly. For a while there are only two specific areas of light in the room.

Oscar, my sins are scarlet and unforgivable. You must help me. Save me from myself. There are so many things inside me – I can't understand them. I have my illusions, live in them, and through their shifting mists and coloured veils, see all things changed. You think life is going to be a brilliant comedy and that I am to be a figure of grace in it. It will be instead a repellent tragedy, whenever I am Nemesis stripped of that mask of Joy and Pleasure by which we both are deceived and led astray.

Bosie rises and moves to the centre of the room. The stage lights come up.

I like yourself have a terrible weakness, though one of an entirely opposite character. It is this, in me hate is always stronger than love. My hatred of my father is of such stature that it entirely outstrips, overwhelms, and overthrows my love for you. By some strange law of the antipathy of similars, my father and I, loathe each other, not because in so many points we are so different, but because in some we were so alike. We share a fascination for the gutter.

Bosie turns away from Oscar's chair.

There are many in my line who have stained their hands in their own blood; my uncle certainly, my grandfather possibly. My elder brother, my poor elder brother, was found on the eve of his marriage, lying dead in a ditch, with his gun discharged beside him. And I am another in the mad, bad line of the Douglas.

He turns to Oscar.

I am the worst friend in the world for you, and this tempts you beyond any reason. You like your characters can resist everything, except temptation.

He turns back to the desk.

My father and I – we are like lovers. We are like lovers who have come to loathe each other because each has discovered in the other, things he despises in himself.

Turning to Oscar, with an incredible look of disgust on his face

He only thinks of his disgusting appetites, his loathsome sensuality. His physical self – a leering ape's face, a squat little hairy body, coarse revolting skin, and his smell – his smell of dung and of urine, of steaming cesspits – I believe that all this is the expression of his soul. Sins of the flesh are nothing. They are maladies for physicians to cure, if they should be cured. Sins of the soul alone are shameful.

In this hideous game of hate, I may throw dice with my father for your soul, and happen to lose. I warn you now because I do care.

> *There is a silence. Bosie snuffs out the candle. The lights fade indicating a passage of time.*

Oscar, listen to this:

Alfred,

It is extremely painful to me to write to you and I decline to receive any answers from you. After your recent hysterical, impertinent letters, I refuse to be annoyed by any more.

Firstly, am I to understand that, having left Oxford as you did with discredit to yourself, the reasons of which were fully explained to me by your tutor, you now intend to loaf and loll about and do nothing? All the time that you were wasting at Oxford I was put off with an assurance that you were eventually to go into the Civil Service or to the Foreign Office or to the Bar. It appears to me that you intend to do nothing. I utterly decline to supply you with the funds to enable you to loaf about. You are preparing a wretched future for yourself.

Secondly, your intimacy with this man, Wilde. It must either cease or I will disown you. I am not going to try and analyse this intimacy and I make no charge; but to my mind to pose as a thing is as bad as to be it. With my own eyes I saw you both in the most loathsome and disgusting relationship. Never in my experience have I seen such a sight as that in your horrible features. No wonder people are talking as they are. Also I now hear on good authority, that his wife is petitioning to divorce him for sodomy and other crimes. If I thought the actual thing was true I should be quite justified in shooting him at sight. These Christian English cowards and men as they call themselves want waking up. Your disgusted so-called father,

Queensberry

39

Bosie tears up the letter, slowly and methodically.
With great casualness he says

That pimp. That lecherous damned pimp.

He moves to his desk.

I shall reply – a concise line that expresses my delicate feelings for him.

On a scrap of the torn letter Bosie scrawls

Dear father – What a funny little man you are.

Bosie laughs and turns to Oscar.

Is that sufficient? Oscar you haven't been listening. What are you staring at?

He moves to the small table beside Oscar's chair
and picks up a visiting card from the Albemarle
Club, an exclusive men's club of which Wilde and
Queensberry were members. There is a moment of
silence.

Why didn't you show this to me sooner? Don't you see? We've got him, got the filthy little beast at last!

Reading the card

To Oscar Wilde – posing as a somdomite.

Bosie laughs uproariously.

And now I know that people with filthy minds can't spell! To Oscar Wilde posing as a SOMDOMITE!

Bosie moves towards Oscar.

He sends cards to your club, Oscar – cards with hideous words on them. London is told that I am associated with a sodomite, and you choose to say nothing. You ignore it out of goodwill. My dearest, if we let this chance escape us now, he will proclaim victory from every Soho stewhouse.

The world will pronounce our guilt by default. People will say Oscar Wilde was terrified by the Marquis of Queensberry. And once my father hears of this he will invent more taunts. He will write to Constance, he will even try and send letters to your infant sons. Nothing can stop him then, unless we take him to court now.

With feverish excitement

Just let me stand in the witness box and expose his wickedness to the world.

Bosie looks at Oscar

Oh don't just sit there snivelling and allow this to pass us by. When you are not on your pedestal you are not interesting.

> *then with a rapid change of mood he kneels by Oscar's chair.*

Oscar, listen to me. If you love me, if you ever loved me, stand by this decision now. Take him to court. We will smash him completely. You will be your Bosie's champion.

> *With great charm and child-like tenderness*

I will remember this above every gift you ever gave me. We can do it my love, we can do it!

> *The lights snap out. Several months pass.*

> *Scene Six. The time is just after Wilde has been sentenced to two years of hard labour after a series of humiliating and grisly trials. In this scene Bosie attempts to relive what went on in those eventful weeks – a period of time that was to haunt him for the rest of his days. As the lights come up on the scene he is reading a letter that he has written in defence of Wilde.*

The Editor
The Review of Reviews

Sir,

I have just read your comments on the Oscar Wilde case in *The Review of Reviews*. I believe you to be a man with a conscience and one who, if he thought a terrible wrong had been done, would not sit with his hands folded and do nothing. Now, sir, you admit the common cant about unnatural offences is not worth anything, you have sufficient philosophy to understand and sufficient boldness to say that to call a thing *unnatural* is not only not necessary to condemn it, but is even to a certain extent to commend it. Everything that diverges from the normal may to a certain extent be called unnatural, genius and beauty among them.

> *Bosie looks up from the letter and addresses the rest directly to the audience.*

And sir, may I ask you if it ever occurred to you to consider the relative deserts of Mr. Oscar Wilde and the man who ruined him, my father, Lord Queensberry? Mr. Oscar Wilde seduced no one, he did no one any harm, he was a kind, generous man, utterly incapable of meanness or cruelty. Lord Queensberry was divorced from my mother, after for twelve years she had silently endured the most horrible suffering at his hands.

He broke her heart, he ruined her health. He has been to beat on the door of her house when she was nearly dying upstairs, he flaunts about with prostitutes and kept women and spends on them the money which he should give to his children.

Last year he induced a girl of seventeen to marry him in a registry office against the wish of her people. On the following day he deserted her, and has since been divorced for a second time. Not content with practising fornication and adultery, he has written pamphlets and given lectures advocating what he calls a sort of polygamy which is neither more nor less than free love. This is the man who has been made into a hero by the English people and the *press,* who is cheered in the streets by the mob, and who has crowned his career by dishonouring and driving out of England his son who now writes to you.

I am, sir, your obedient servant,
Alfred Douglas

Throwing the letter down, he confronts the audience.

Now the world must give the devil his due and granting for the sake of argument that I am an exceptional young scoundrel who has ruined Oscar Wilde's life, the world still has no right to call me a coward.

He has been subjected to three trials by ignorant brutes. His counsel refused to let me testify against my father and so – we are lost. All trials are trials for one's life just as all sentences are sentences of death and his sentence has been published in every catch-penny rag in England. It has been said – but no more details – "details," as Oscar once remarked, "are always vulgar."

Still Nemesis has worked a detailed pattern. Our charade owed nothing to chance. We are the zanies of sorrow – our emotions on shameful display. Where is the nobility of this public pain?

Oh but I remember those trial days of shame had moments of triumph, when feasting with panthers seemed a desirable luxury.

Must I remember?

Pause

Yes – everything that is realised is right.

The second trial dragged on and on. Oscar didn't care. And it wasn't until a prosecuting attorney sneeringly asked "Mr. Wilde, would you explain to the court what is the love that dare not speak its name?", that he was moved enough to answer, "Yes, Mr. Prosecutor, I will.

Bosie moves to the centre of the room and looks directly at Oscar's chair while reciting the following speech.

"The Love that dare not speak its name in this century is such a great affection of an elder for a younger man as there was between David and

Jonathan, such as Plato made the very basis of his philosophy. It is that deep spiritual affection that is as pure as it is perfect. It dictates and pervades great works of art like those of Shakespeare and Michelangelo. In this century it is misunderstood, so much misunderstood that it may be described as the Love that dare not speak its name, and on account of it, I am placed where I am now. It is beautiful, it is fine, it is the noblest form of affection. There is nothing unnatural about it. It is intellectual and it repeatedly exists between an elder man and younger man, when the elder man has intellect and the younger man has all the joy, hope, and glamour of life before him. That it should be so the world does not understand. The world mocks at it, and sometimes puts one in the pillory for it."

Silence. Bosie addresses the chair where Oscar used to sit.

Oscar, did you hear the thunderous applause in the courtroom?

He turns back to speak to the audience.

They ordered a re-trial, the third one. And the miracle did not occur. It was brutal, shabby and explicit. Edward Carson, the prosecutor, produced a trump card of a most vulgar nature. His witnesses were boys who had been procured for Oscar.

One can imagine Carson purring with innocence, as he led Oscar on to say the words that damned us irrevocably. They were talking about a servant of mine at Oxford. "Did you Mr. Wilde, ever kiss this person?" Oscar laughed mock-ruefully: "Oh dear no. He was a peculiarly plain boy. He was unfortunately extremely ugly. I pitied him for it." And Carson's face was ablaze with triumph as he quietly said: "Was *that* why you did not kiss him?"

The words hang heavily in the air. There is a silence. With slow deliberation, Bosie pronounces Wilde's sentence aloud.

"Oscar Wilde, the crime of which you have been convicted is so bad that one has to put stern restraint upon oneself, from describing in language which I would rather not use, the sentiments which must rise to the breast of every man of honour who has heard the details of these terrible trials. It is no use for me to address you, people who can do these things must be dead to all sense of shame, and one cannot hope to produce any effect upon them. It is the worst case that I have ever tried. That you, Wilde, have been the centre of a circle of extensive corruption among young men, it is impossible to doubt. I shall under such circumstances be expected to pass the severest sentence that the law of England allows. In my judgment it is wholly inadequate for such a case as this. The sentence of the court is that you are to be imprisoned and kept to hard labour for two years."

The lights dim and Bosie moves slowly to the centre of the room.

Outside the Old Bailey, respectable citizens and painted whores danced in joy at the sentence. One harlot yelled from her house as Oscar passed by, "He'll 'ave his 'air cut reg'lar now."

And Oscar's Muse of Laughter would not go away. Upon being told in exaggerated detail of Oscar's perversions, an old gentleman at the Albemarle Club muttered, "I don't care what he does, as long as he doesn't do it in the streets and frighten the horses."

And Bosie laughs bitterly at the memory.

I saw him every day in Holloway prison - an incomplete nightmare. Human ingenuity could devise nothing more malignant; we were herded into boxes rather like those in a pawnshop. There was a whole row of boxes, each occupied by a visitor. Opposite facing us was the prisoner we were visiting. Our two lines were separated by a corridor about a yard wide. We shouted to make our voices heard. A warder tramped up and down between us. The din was unbearable.

There was an elderly woman beside me. With grace she wore the tatters of respectability. One eye of hers was sewn shut, a black hole in a pale face. She was crying softly, and said to her son of seventeen or thereabouts: "Be good, Jamie. Say your prayers. I love you. Goodbye."

They needed more money, so he stole and was caught and will be shut away from the world for the rest of his mother's life. And we were part of all that. The image of her doom haunts me. Oscar is rather deaf, so there was nothing for us to say. We looked at each other and the only message that hammered its way into our hearts was through tears, then silence, and then a clanging bell. Our quarter of an hour was up.

> *There is a silence. Bosie prepares to leave, then*
> *suddenly stops. All the lights, save a spot*
> *illuminating his face, go out.*

Oh but I remember – I remember the first time we made love. I wrote a sonnet about it. Oscar wrote a letter.

My own boy,

Your sonnet is quite lovely, and it is a marvel that those red rose-leaf lips of yours should have been made no less for the music of song than for madness of kisses.

Your slim gilt soul walks between passion and poetry. I know Hyacinthus, whom Apollo loved so madly, was you in Greek days. Why are you alone in London, and when do you go to Salisbury? Do go there to cool your hands in the grey twilight of Gothic things, and come back here whenever you like. It is a lovely place, it only lacks you. But go to Salisbury first.

Always with undying love,
Yours, Oscar

The spot slowly fades.

End of Act One.

Act Two

*A few years after the death of Oscar Wilde in
1900. The set is stripped down to give a feeling of
barrenness to the room. The lights come up to
reveal Bosie Douglas studying his features in a
hand-mirror. It is not the young Dorian Gray of
the first act that the audience sees, but an older,
rather sour-looking, replica. Slowly he speaks:*

No you are not Dorian Gray after all. There is decay and sourness in this
visage. I thrive on a truth-telling glass. The past memory is sweeter.

He puts down the mirror.

I remember the first time I met him; there was the warning scent of the
passion-flower, the deceptive lightness of a cucumber sandwich. I see it over
and over again – within me, locked in crystal. I see our words, our
movements, – walking together in the moonlight of Naples, or laughing,
excited and surrounded by the ancient passion of Egypt. I see a flashing sea,
a sunny hillside. He is coming to join me, but I cannot quite make out the
face above the body. I wait. The sun and sea fade. I stare instead at the
cold walls of his cell. And he is not there. Oscar? Oscar?

Pause

Put yourself behind me. I served the memory for years. Let me exorcise it,
begin again. Since he died I see him every night.

Bosie sits at his desk and tries to finish a sonnet
that he has started to compose.

I dreamed of him last night, I saw his face
All radiant and unshadowed of distress
And as of old in music measureless
I heard his golden voice and marked him trace
Wonders that might have been. . . .

He cannot continue. A brief silence.

I decided to return to England to visit him in Reading Gaol. I was told
that his correspondence and visitors were strictly limited. He desired that I
should neither write to him nor visit him. So determined to follow out his
wishes, I waited until he could write or send to me. I tried to show the love,
which he must have known I had for him, by the most difficult of all ways,
waiting.

Bosie picks up De Profundis, *the long letter that*
Oscar Wilde wrote to him while in prison.

Dear Bosie,

After long and fruitless waiting I have determined to write to you myself,
as much for your sake as mine, as I would not like to think that I had
passed through two long years of imprisonment without ever having received
a single line from you, or any news or message even, except such as gave me
pain. Our illfated and most lamentable friendship has ended in ruin and
public infamy for me, yet the memory of our ancient affection is often with
me, and the thought that loathing, bitterness and contempt should forever
take that place in my heart once held by love is very sad to me.

I will begin by telling you that I blame myself terribly. As I sit here in
this dark cell in convict clothes, a disgraced and ruined man, I blame
myself. In the perturbed and fitful nights of anguish, in the long

monotonous days of pain, it is myself I blame. I blame myself for allowing an unintellectual friendship, a friendship whose primary aim was not the creation and contemplation of beautiful things to entirely dominate my life. From the first there was too wide a gap between us.

Those incessant scenes that seemed to be almost physically necessary to you, and in which your mind and body grew distorted and you became a thing as terrible to look at as to listen to: that dreadful mania you inherit from your father, the mania for writing revolting and loathsome letters: your entire lack of any control over your emotions – these, I say, were the origin and causes of my fatal yielding to you in your daily increasing demands. You wore me out.

Those of my friends who really desired my welfare implored me to retire abroad, and not to face an impossible trial. You imputed mean motives to them for giving me such advice, and cowardice to me for listening to it. You forced me to stay, to brazen it out if possible, in the box by absurd and silly perjuries. At the end, I was of course arrested and your father became the hero of the hour. Your father will always live among the kind, pure-minded parents of Sunday school literature, your place is with the Infant Samuel, and in the lowest mire of Malebolge I sit between Gilles de Retz and the Marquis de Sade.

The gods are strange. It is not of our vices only they make instruments to scourge us. They bring us to ruin through what in us is good, gentle, humane, loving. But for my pity and affection for you and yours, I would not be weeping in this terrible place.

You can understand – can you not? – a little of what I am suffering. Some paper describing the dress rehearsal of one of my plays, spoke of you as following me about like my shadow: the memory of our friendship is the shadow that walks with me here; there is nothing that happened in those ill-starred years that I cannot recreate in that chamber of the brain which is set apart for grief or for despair: every strained note of your voice, every twitch and gesture of your nervous hands, every bitter word, every poisonous phrase comes back to me. I remember the street or river down which we passed, the wall or woodland that surrounds us, at what figure on the dial stood the hands of the clock, which way went the wings of the wind, the shape and colour of the moon.

There is, I know, one answer to all that I have said to you, and that is that you loved me: that all through those two and a half years during which the Fates were weaving into one scarlet pattern the threads of our divided lives, you really loved me.

How clearly I saw it then, as now, I need not tell you. But I said to myself, "At all costs, I must keep Love in my heart. If I go into prison without Love what will become of my soul?" The letters I wrote to you at that time from Holloway were the efforts to keep Love as the dominant note of my own nature. I could if I had chosen have torn you to pieces with bitter reproaches. I could have rent you with maledictions. I could have held up a mirror to you and shown you such an image of yourself that you would not have recognized it as your own till you found it mimicking back your gestures of horror, and then you would have known whose shape it was, and hated it and yourself forever.

The messenger of Death has brought me his tidings and gone his way, and in entire solitude, and isolated from all that could give me comfort, or suggest relief, I have had to bear the intolerable burden of misery and remorse that the memory of my mother placed upon me and places on me still. Hardly had that wound been dulled, not healed, by time, when violent and bitter and harsh letters come to me from my wife through her solicitor. I am, at once, taunted and threatened with poverty. That I can bear. I can school myself to worse than that. But my two children are taken from me by legal procedure. That is and always will remain to me a source of infinite distress, of infinite pain, of grief without end or limit. That the law should decide, and take upon itself to decide, that I am one unfit to be with my own children is something quite horrible to me.

I remember when I was at Oxford saying to one of my friends – as we were strolling round Magdalen's narrow bird-haunted walks one morning in June before I took my degree – that I wanted to eat the fruit of all the trees in the garden of the world, and that I was going out into the world with that passion in my soul. And so indeed I went out, and so I lived. My only mistake was that I confined myself so exclusively to the trees of what seemed to me the sungilt side of the garden and shunned the other side for its shadow and its gloom. I don't regret for a single moment having lived for pleasure. I did it to the full as one should do everything that one does to the full. There was no pleasure I did not experience. I threw the pearl of my soul into a cup of wine. I went down the primrose path to the sound of flutes. I lived on honeycomb. But to have continued the same life would have been limiting. I had to pass on. The other half of the garden had its secrets for me also.

Everything about my tragedy has been hideous, mean, repellent, lacking in style. Our very dress makes us grotesques. We are specially designed to appeal to the sense of humour. On November 13, 1895 I was brought to Reading from London. From two o'clock till half past two on that day I had to stand on the centre platform of Clapham Junction in convict dress, and handcuffed for the world to look at. I had been taken out of the hospital ward without a moment's notice being given to me. Of all possible objects I was the most grotesque. And when people saw me they laughed. Each train as it came up swelled the audience. Nothing could exceed their amusement. And that was, of course, before they knew who I was. As soon as they had been informed they laughed still more. For half an hour I stood there in the grey November rain surrounded by a jeering mob.

For a year after that was done to me I wept every day at the same hour for the same space of time. Now remember, that is not such a tragic thing as it possibly sounds to you. To us who lie in prison tears are a part of every day's experience. A day in prison on which a man does not weep is a day on which his heart is hard, not a day on which his heart is happy.

And man's very highest moment is, I have no doubt at all, when he kneels in the dust and beats his breast, and tells all the sins of his life. And so with you. You would be much happier if you let your mother know a little of your life: from yourself. And do not allow sentimentality to hinder you.

Remember that the sentimentalist is invariably a cynic at heart. Indeed sentimentality is merely the bank holiday for cynicism. And as delightful as cynicism is from its intellectual side, in itself it can never be more than the perfect philosophy for the man without a soul, for to the true cynic, nothing is ever revealed.

And incomplete, and imperfect as I am, yet from me you still have much to gain. You came to me once long ago – do you remember – to learn the pleasure of life and the pleasure of art. Well, perhaps now I am chosen to teach you something much more wonderful: the meaning of sorrow and its beauty.

Your affectionate friend,
Oscar Wilde

In the ensuing silence, Bosie lets the letter slip from his fingers to the floor. He looks at his hand as he begins the next speech.

The last time I saw him, before I left for France, he kissed the ends of my fingers through an iron grating at Holloway Prison, and he begged me to let nothing in the world alter my attitude and my conduct towards him. He wrote to me in the same strain many, many times and he warned me that all sorts of influences would be brought to bear upon me to make me change. I will not change now. I decline to listen to anything that he said while he was in prison. If he really meant what he said and if he was really not mad, he is not the person I remember and he is not Oscar, the Oscar to whom I shall in memory always be faithful, and who belonged to me quite absolutely. When lovers quarrel, they return to each other their letters and presents. Oscar and I were lovers, but we had not quarrelled after he had come out of Reading Gaol and as I had not asked for a return to my letters and my presents, he could not ask for his. But I do not believe *De Profundis*, I regard it as non-existent. I attribute it simply to an evil and lying spirit which then inhabited Oscar's body, a spirit born in an English prison, out of English prison discipline, and which I hoped in spite of everything to have ultimately cast out of him. But even if I never did cast it out of him, even if Oscar's body was always secretly inhabited by this thing, even if at the last meeting I really said good-bye to him forever, I still have loved my own Oscar, the real one, and I should always refuse to take any notice of English prison spirits.

> *Bosie looks over at Oscar's chair and as he begins to address Oscar, the "Special" which had been out since the beginning of Act Two comes on. It stays on for the rest of the Act, indicating that Oscar's spirit is somehow locked into the room, while Bosie exorcises the guilt surrounding his memories of the last few days of their relationship.*

Oscar, if only you could understand that though you were in prison, you were still the court, the jury, the judge of my life and that I was waiting and hoping for some sign that I was to go on living. I am inordinately conceited and have a great opinion of myself as a poet, I think myself a very great poet,

He looks at the unfinished poem.

or rather I think I was a great poet. If I thought I could have gone on writing splendid works of art I would have lived for that, but I knew the power had left me and I had nothing in the world to live for, except you.

> *The lights and mood brighten. Bosie moves to the centre of the room and addresses the audience directly.*

He was released from gaol May 1897, and among the people who had gathered to meet him was his old friend, Ada Leverson, the Sphinx.

"We all felt acutely embarrassed," she admitted, "at the thought of seeing Oscar again. But when Oscar came in, he at once put us at our ease. He came in with the dignity of a king returning from exile. He came in talking, laughing, smoking a cigarette, with waved hair, a flower in his buttonhole – and his first words were: 'Sphinx! Sphinxes are minions of the moon, yet you rise before dawn to greet me. And Sphinx how marvellous of you to know exactly the right hat to wear at seven o'clock in the morning to meet a friend who has been away. You can't have got up, you must have sat up'.

"He talked on lightly for some time, then he wrote a letter, and sent it in a cab to a Roman Catholic retreat, asking if he might retire there for six months or so. While waiting, he lounged in a corner of the sofa smoking cigarette after cigarette; presently he said: 'Sphinx, do you know one of the dreadful punishments that happens to people who have been away? They are not allowed to read the *Daily Chronicle*. Did you know that? Coming along here I begged to be allowed to read it in the train. Impossible. Couldn't be done, my captors asserted. Then I suggested that I might be allowed to read it upside down. This to my enormous astonishment they consented to. And so, dear Sphinx, all the way from Reading to London I read the *Daily Chronicle* upside down, and I never enjoyed it so much in all my life. It is the only way to read newspapers'.

"The man returned with the letter, everyone looked away while Oscar read it. They replied that they could not accept him in the Catholic retreat on impulse of moment. It must be seriously thought of for at least a year. In fact they refused him. Oscar broke down and sobbed bitterly. He left for France that same afternoon. He never set foot in England again."

Brief pause. Bosie picks up the train of his thoughts again.

What we never realized then was the fun of being with Oscar. Not his epigrams or more studied humour, but his continuous light-heartedness and love of laughter. Everyone felt gay and carefree in his company. He wasn't a funny man looking for chances to make jokes, he bubbled all the time with happy humour, and he encouraged it in those with him. Everyone talked a little better with Oscar than with anyone else. The worst of *De Profundis* is that it makes our friendship seem a solemn sort of thing crossed with terrible quarrels. But we were laughing most of the time – often at one another. There were whole days when we laughed our way through. I remember going into Torquay for breakfast once, I forget why now, and being told by the waiter that there was some nice fish. "If you knew the breeding habits of fish," said Oscar, "you would scarcely call them nice." Not a remark to treasure perhaps, but one that led us into endless absurdities. That's what simple unintellectual people loved about Oscar. He could make them laugh. And that kind of humour is incommunicable. It's like trying to convey the qualities of a really great actor. You can record a man's most brilliant remarks and say, "He was a marvellous conversationalist." But you can't really show him as he was. It's all down on the passing moment, spontaneous, fleeting, not to be set down in words.

And Oscar never had any regard for consistency. It was one of what he

60

called the Seven Deadly Virtues. Obviously he did not take *De Profundis* seriously, for a few months later he wrote:

The letter is recited from memory.

My own darling boy,

I just send you a line to say that I feel my only hope of doing beautiful work in Art is being with you, and you can really re-create in me that energy and sense of joyous power on which Art depends. Everyone is furious for me going back to you, but they don't understand us. I feel it is only with you that I can do anything at all. Do remake my ruined life for me, and then our friendship will have a different meaning to the world. I wish we had not parted at all. There are such wide abysses of space and land between us. But we love each other.

Goodnight dear.
Ever yours, Oscar

In a hushed voice, Bosie continues.

We met that same year at Posilippo in Naples. Poor Oscar cried when I met him. We walked about all day arm in arm, or hand in hand, and were very happy. And our respective families were shocked. Oscar's friends were enraged. How could he re-unite with the one person instrumental in his ruin? Oscar, of course, provided the reply:

"Much that you say is right, but still you leave out of consideration the great love I have for Bosie. I love him and have always loved him. He ruined my life and for that reason I seem destined to love him more: and now I shall do lovely work. Bosie is himself a poet, far the first poet of all the young poets of England, an exquisite artist in lyric and ballad. It is to a poet that I am going back. So when people say how dreadful of me to return to Bosie, do say no. Say that I love him, that he is a poet, and that after all whatever my life may have been ethically, it has always been *romantic*. And Bosie is my romance. My romance is a tragedy of course, but it is nonetheless a romance, and he loves me very dearly, more than he loves or can love anyone else, and without him my life was dreary. So stick up for us and be nice.

Your friend,
Oscar"

A brief silence. Bosie moves towards Oscar's chair.

But there was no real desire left within him to create lovely works of art. I asked him why and he said:

"Because I have written all that I was to write. I wrote when I did not know the meaning of Life, now that I know the meaning of Life I have no more to write. Life cannot be written, life can only be lived. I have lived."

The "Oscar Special" goes out slowly. Bosie stands in silence. The lights begin to dim gradually. When he speaks his voice is dull and bitter.

And the herb that time and time again had soothed every hurt, simple human laughter, happy, happy, laughter had gone. There was something sad too, about meeting him again. For two years we had imagined our reunion in hysterical lovely visions - but the time gone by had altered body, mind, and soul, into another shape. The halves did not fit. His teeth had decayed and he was worried about money; my freshness had gone and I talked too much about too little. Even our tired amours with young flesh, the dark rough diamonds of Italy, did little to bring back the flame. A tower of ivory had been assailed by the foul thing.

Bosie picks up the green carnation that has lain on Oscar's chair. He looks at it with great regret. Quietly, he continues

And yet finally, I broke the silence surrounding his pen. This time I readily agreed that he should not dedicate this work to me, or to any of his friends, but to the English soldier – I forget his name – who inspired it. Oscar had never exchanged a single word with him, but day after day he had seen the anguish of this man who was sentenced to hang for the murder of his own wife. And to him Oscar dedicated *The Ballad of Reading Gaol.*

The lighting on the Ballad *follows the intensity of mood that is quite strongly dictated by the poem. The general lighting on the stage grows darker until its eventual blackout. Two spots, one illuminating the full figure of Bosie Douglas, the other illuminating just his face, glow in the darkness. Towards the end of the poem the larger spot fades out, leaving us the image of Bosie's face.*

He did not wear his scarlet coat,
For blood and wine are red,
And blood and wine were on his hands
When they found him with the dead,
The poor dead woman whom he loved,
And murdered in her bed.

He walked amongst the Trial Men
In a suit of shabby grey;
A cricket cap was on his head,
And his step seemed light and gay;

But I never saw a man who looked
So wistfully at the day.

I never saw a man who looked
With such a wistful eye
Upon that little tent of blue
Which prisoners call the sky,
And at every drifting cloud that went
With sails of silver by.

I walked with other souls in pain,
Within another ring,
And was wondering if the man had done
A great or little thing,
When a voice behind me whispered low,
"That fellow's got to swing."

Dear Christ! the very prison walls
Suddenly seemed to reel,
And the sky above my head became
Like a casque of scorching steel;
And though I was a soul in pain,
My pain I could not feel.

I only knew what hunted thought
Quickened his step, and why
He looked upon the garish day
With such a wistful eye;
The man had killed the thing he loved,
And so he had to die.

Yet each man kills the thing he loves,
By each let this be heard,
Some do it with a bitter look
Some with a flattering word,
The coward does it with a kiss,
The brave man with a sword.

That night the empty corridors
Were full of forms of fear,
And up and down the iron town
Stole feet we could not hear,
And through the bars that hide the stars
White faces seemed to peer.

At last I saw the shadowed bars,
Like a lattice wrought in lead,
Move right across the white-washed wall
That faced my three-plank bed,
And I knew that somewhere in the world
God's dreadful dawn was red.

With sudden shock the prison clock
Smote on the shivering air,
And from all the gaol rose up a wail
Of impotent despair,
Like the sound that frightened marshes hear
From some leper in his lair.

And as one sees most fearful things
In a crystal of a dream,

We saw the greasy hempen rope
Hooked to the blackened beam,
And heard the prayer the hangman's snare
Strangled into a scream.

And all the woe that moved him so
That he gave that bitter cry,
And the wild regrets, and the bloody sweats
None knew so well as I:
For he who lives more lives than one
More deaths than one must die.

The warders strutted up and down,
And watched their herd of brutes,
Their uniforms were spick and span,
And they wore their Sunday suits,
But we knew the work they had been at,
By the quicklime on their boots.

For where a grave had opened wide,
There was no grave at all:
Only a stretch of mud and sand
By the hideous prison wall.
And a little heap of burning lime,
That the man should have his pall.

Some love too little, some too long,
Some sell, and others buy;
Some do the deed with many tears,
And some without a sigh:

For each man kills the thing he loves,
Yet each man does not die.

He does not die a death of shame
On a day of dark disgrace,
Nor have a noose about his neck,
Nor a cloth upon his face,
Nor drop feet foremost through the floor
Into an empty space.

He does not wake at dawn to see
Dread figures throng his room,
The shivering Chaplain robed in white,
The Sheriff stern with gloom,
And the Governor all in shiny black
With the yellow face of Doom.

So with curious eyes and sick surmise
We watched him day by day,
And wondered if each one of us
Would end the self-same way,
For none can tell to what red Hell
His sightless soul may stray.

We sewed the sacks, we broke the stones,
We turned the dusty drill:
We banged the tins, and bawled the hymns,
And sweated on the mill:
But in the heart of every man
Terror was lying still.

So still it lay that every day
Crawled like a weed-clogged wave:
And we forgot the bitter lot
That waits for fool and knave,
Till once, as we tramped in from work,
We passed an open grave.

Then back we went with soul intent
On Death and Dread and Doom:
The hangman with his little bag,
Went shuffling through the gloom.
And each man trembled as he crept
Into his numbered tomb.

For he has a pall, this wretched man,
Such as few men can claim:
Deep down below a prison yard,
Naked for greater shame,
He lies, with fetters on each foot,
Wrapped in a sheet of flame!

And all the while the burning lime
Eats flesh and bone away,
It eats the brittle bone by night,
And the soft flesh by day.
It eats the flesh and bone by turn
But it eats the heart away.

Yet all is well; he has but passed
To life's appointed bourne

And alien tears will fill for him
Pity's long broken urn
For his mourners will be outcast men
And outcasts always mourn.

In Reading Gaol by Reading Town
There is a pit of shame,
And in it lies a broken man
Eaten by teeth of flame,
In a burning winding sheet he lies
And his grave has got no name.

And there till Christ call forth the dead,
In silence let him lie:
No need to waste the foolish tear,
Or heave the windy sigh:
The man had killed the thing he loved,
And so he had to die.

And all men kill the thing they love,
By all let this be heard,
Some do it with a bitter look,
Some with a flattering word,
The coward does it with a kiss,
The brave man with a sword!

A long silence as Bosie struggles with his emotions.
He lifts the green carnation that he has held with
him throughout the Ballad, *into the pin-spot.*
In a hushed whisper he speaks the last few lines.

You know, my life with him was always a contradiction in extremity.

I dreamed of him last night, I saw his face
All radiant and unshadowed of distress
And as of old in music measureless
I heard his golden voice and marked him trace
Wonders that might have been inarticulate
And voiceless thoughts like murdered singing birds,
And so I woke - and knew, that he was dead.

The light snaps out.